WHAT IF I'M WRONG

Prince of Peace

WHAT IF I'M WRONG

TABLE OF CONTENT

INTERDUCTION

Life is a journey filled with difficulties challenges, and triumphs, it is a constant battle between our inner strength, and weaknesses. While we all aspire to live a life of purpose and resilience. There are habits that often hold us back from reaching our full potential, in this transformative journey we will explore nine habits that make you weak and learn how to overcome them. Using the principles of stoicism and ancient Greek philosophy, founded by Zeno of Citium, in the early third century BC, offers timeless wisdom that can help us, navigate the complexities of modern life stoicism. Teaches us to focus on what we can control, to cultivate virtue like wisdom, courage, self-discipline, and to accept the inevitable challenges of life with grace and resilience. As we delve into these eight habits, remember that self-awareness is the first step towards transformation, by recognising and acknowledging these habits, within ourselves. We can begin the journey of replacing them with stoic principles, which will empower us to lead a life of strength, purpose, and inner peace. Habit #1 procrastination of time epictetus said, the key is to keep Company only with people who uplift you, whose presence calls forth your best procrastination. The act of postponing tasks and responsibilities is a habit that plagues many of us, it weakens our resolve, hinders our progress, and robs us of precious time, which could be invested in personal growth, and meaningful endeavours. The historic remedy for procrastination lies in the concept of carpe diem or seizing the day in stoicism. The focus is on the present moment and making the most of its procrastination, on the other hand is rooted in anxiety, about the future, or the discomfort of the task at hand, to overcome this habit, we must adopt A stoic mindset.

INTERDUCTION

Remind ourselves, that the only time we truly have control, over is now Epictetus A stoic philosopher, advised us to focus on what is within our control. Let go of what is not procrastination, often arises from fixating on the potential outcomes, or the difficulties of a task, rather than simply acting by adopting the stoic principle, of focusing on the process rather than the outcome. We can break free from the chains of procrastination, start by setting small manageable goals, and consistently work towards them, embrace the discomfort and uncertainty, of the present moment. For it is in these moments of challenge, that we grow and develop the strength to face larger tasks. Remember that time is a finite resource, and each day you delay is a day last forever, that will empower us to lead a life of strength, purpose, and inner peace. Habit #2 negative self-talk Marcus Aurelius said, our life is what our thoughts make it, the way we speak to ourselves has a profound impact on our self-esteem, confidence, and overall well-being. Negative self-talk is a habit, which weakens us by eroding our self-belief, and preventing us from realising our true potential. Stoicism teaches us to take control of our thoughts and replace negativity with rationality and self-compassion. Marcus Aurelius one of the most renowned historic philosophers, and Roman emperors emphasised. the importance of monitoring our inner dialogue, he believed that our perception of the world is shaped by our thoughts, and therefore we must strive to maintain a positive and rational mindset, to combat negative self-talk, begin by observing your thoughts without judgement. Notice when self-criticism or self-doubt creeps in and challenge these thoughts with rationality.

INTERDUCTION

Ask yourself whether these thoughts are based on evidence, or merely products of fear, and insecurity stoicism encourages us to practise self-compassion, treating ourselves with the same kindness, and understanding that we would offer to a friend. Facing an analogous situation instead of berating yourself for mistakes, or perceived shortcomings. Focus on what you can learn from them, and how you can improve as you replace negative self-talk with stoic principles of rationality, and self-compassion. You will discover an inner strength, and resilience that will empower you to face life's challenges with confidence, and grace. Habit #3 avoiding challenges if you want to improve yourself, be willing to let others think you are foolish and ignorant. Avoiding challenges and staying in your comfort zone is a habit, which weakens your development and potential, it prevents you from developing patience courage and adaptability, to new situations. Stoic philosophy teaches us to face discomfort and difficulties, as opportunities for self-improvement Epictetus, believe that personal growth and self-mastery often come from facing challenges, and pushing our boundaries facing the avoidance of challenges, is considered important for personal development and self-improvement. Stoics believed that by voluntarily facing tricky situations, we developed patience enhance our morality, and gain a deeper understanding of ourselves, and the world around us.

Here is the big challenge of life, you can have more than you have got, because you can become more, than you are, that's the challenge of course, side of the coin reeds, unless you change how you are, you will always have what you got. I have found in my experience, that income does not far exceed personal development. Now sometimes income takes a lucky jump, but sure enough unless you grow, out where it is, it will usually come back, where you are life, has strange ways. If somebody hands you $1,000,000, best you become a millionaire quickly, so you get to keep the money, otherwise shown up it will disappear. Somebody once said, if you took all the money in the world, divide it up equally among everybody, it would soon all be back in the same pockets. Success is something you attract, not something you pursue, success is looking for a good, place to stay, so instead of going after it, you work on yourself personal development. The major question to ask on the +-orb, is not what you are getting, the major question to ask, on the job is what you are becoming question is not what I am getting paid here, the big question is what I am becoming here. Because turn happiness is not contained, in what you get happiness is contained in what you become. That is our major subject for tonight First well development of all the assignments, Mr self-gave me at age 25, this was the most difficult, in fact I am still working on this one. It is an unending challenge to see, what you can become.

A LIST OF GOLS   PAGE 2.

The next subject is called basic gloves, and it is good to study, the basics and I call these basics primarily, because they come from the Bible. Now I am not a theologian or a minister, and that will be apparent, but Mr self-taught me, that the Bible was a good textbook, for ideas, stories, and success, equations how to live the better life. I found out that was true, he also taught me that the Bible is as practical, as it is spiritual and I found out true if you look at your bank account, in your income and you are not happy. There here is several places in the Bible, to check to see what the hacks wrong. So, you can make the changes, and we are going to cover some of those in this book, and it called basics. Next Sunday are my favourite setting goals self-taught me how to set goals, what a favour that was morning at breakfast. Shortly after I met him, he said Jim let me see your current list of goals and let us go over and talk about it. He said that is the best way I can help you get a better direction, started I said I do not have a list, he said Well is it out in the car, or home somewhere, I said no Sir I do not have a list anywhere. He said Well young man, who is where we got to start, he said I can tell you right now, if you do not have a list of your goals with you, he said, I can guess your bank balance within a few $100. Which he did that got my attention, my bank balance would change, if I had a list of goals he said drastically. At that day I became a willing student, how to set goals and sure enough learning to set goals changed my life. And I often wondered why no one had ever taught me, how to set goals up until age 25, I went to high school, but if they offered it, I missed it, I went to college for a year never heard it, I work for sears really in all its ears, never taught it how to set goals. So here I am age 25 married my family starting, I've been to college I'm working, and I still don't know how to set goals. But fortunately, when I was 25, I met the man who taught me out, and it revolutionised my whole life economically, socially, personally, it's incredible. so, I want to share with you tonight what Mr show shared with me, how to set goals it can be a life changer.

ATTITUDE DISEASES PAGE 3.

The next subject is the negative part of the seminar, this part negative, so we got to talk about the negative and this subject is called diseases of attitude. There's a lot of things that can wreck your chances to do well, we live in a rather dangerous world. So, you got to be not only wise, but you also got to be careful attitude diseases are just as bad, as physical diseases, right high blood pressure heart trouble, I mean a lot of things lace your chances to do well. So, you have got to be careful, and attitude diseases are deadly, I mean they'll destroy all the good things you start. So, we'll go through those attitude diseases, how to spot him how to look for what they are, and the cure and I'm a pro on these because I've had them all. So, I can give you excellent advice on these. my subject we're going to consider tonight is called the endure life, around David turns your life around and under this subject, we're going to talk about attitude diseases, which can change your life.

YOUR EMOTIONS PAGE 4.

Human beings are emotional creatures and emotions are powerful, for life change now of course emotions are so powerful, they can go either way on your emotions can either build or destroy, so you really must employ emotions properly. We call civilization the intelligent management of human emotions, if you can intelligently apply your emotions in the right direction, no telling what could happen, could turn your life around. One day would be sufficient, so we will talk about those OK. Now that is a lot to cover in one evening, but we will keep at it here see if we can get it all done. I would like to have you now jot down the theme of the seminar every seminar should have a theme. We have got one about literature you happen to notice, that if you did not for your notes here it is the theme of the seminar. I was like this the major key your better future is you, that is the theme of our seminar tonight. The major key to your better future is you, so that it reads the major key to your better future is you. Now my first suggestion is transfer this to a card, or something where you can put it up where you can see it, every day preferably put it up where you can see, that the beginning of the day before you got to put the day together. This is a good phrase just to glance at to keep in mind, as you are putting the day together, it's called the silent seminar. If you just let this talk to you, during the day I found it to be tremendously helpful. The major key to your better future, is you for a big share of my life. Now I did not have this one quite figured out, among a lot of things. I did not have quite figured out many things, used to puzzle me back in those early days. I used to wonder why two people could work for the same company one makes twice as much money.

HOW MUCH DO YOUR WORTH PAGE 5.

Now see that used to puzzle me, and they were the same age graduated from the same school, live in the same community, work for the same company, with the same product in the same services. They have the same traffic the same problems, and one makes 1000 a month, the other makes 2000 a month. Now that was my puzzling question why this extensive list would be the same, and the money twice as much I asked, what is the difference between 1000 a month, and 2000 a month, and I do not mean 1000 a month right I could figure that out. But what makes the difference why would one person do twice as well, three times as well speaking economically. Now I know there is more than one way to do well, I understand that but in this little narrow area, called compensation what is the difference, well back then with my faulty thinking, I am trying to reason it out make some of the difference right. Some people do better because they have more time, I used to say how we got to be able to do well, he has a lot of time, if I had all his time, I could do well. Now that has got to be done, right, number one you cannot get somebody else's time, he said you know if I had some extra time, I could make some extra money, I said then forget it there is not any extra time. When the clock strikes 12 midnight, that about wraps it up, right, you can look around the gongs here for little more, but it's over said to the guy, when you're doing these are looking for extra time, see they'll come and take you away, right. There is not any more time, you cannot get more time which you cannot. What could you get more of it would be effective in economic results, and here is the keyword, make it a part of your notes, we are going to consider it tonight. The word is value can I have a little phrase for your notes value, makes the difference in results value makes the difference, you cannot get more time, but you can create more value. Now here is the first lesson of economics, everybody should learn it from the time they're old enough to understand, what a dollar means, how to earn one how to get one how to keep one, what to do with it first lesson of economics. We primarily get paid for value, that's lesson 1, bringing value to the marketplace, that's how you get paid, you don't get paid for the time, I know it takes time to bring value to the marketplace, but you get paid for the value, not the time. Now since that's true here's one of the key questions of the evening, is it possible to become twice as valuable, at the marketplace and make twice as much money, at the same time could you become three times as valuable, make three times as much money at the same time is that possible, the answer is yes.

YOU GOT TO CHANGE FOR CHANGE TO COME PAGE 6.

if and it is always, if right life is known as the big if, Harry Truman once said life is unsure, how to and here's the big if. We are going to consider it tonight, it is possible to do much better at the marketplace, if you go to work primarily on yourself, and that is the theme of our seminar tonight, learning to work primarily on yourself. People have asked me for the last 24 years, how do you develop an above average income, and the answer is become an above average person develop, an above average. Handshake some people want to be successful, they do not even work on their handshake as easy as that, would be to start on they let it slide. They do not understand developing above average smile, developing above average excitement, developing above average interest in other people developing above average intensity to win. See that will change everything, one of the most frustrating experiences in life, is looking for an above average job with above average pay, without becoming an above average person, it is called restoration. Mr self-gave me the greatest advice, he gave me when I first met him, he said Jim if you want to be wealthy and happy the rest of your life, just learned this lesson. Well, he said learn to work harder on yourself than you do on your job, probably what are the most important clues along with so many things, he taught me, but this was in those early days. Mr Self-is very kind, but he was also very abrupt that is interesting questions to ask, I'm giving him a little run day rundown one day on how things haven't worked out for me, I've got the answer for you if you will listen carefully, and listen carefully I did that day, and for the next five years somebody's wealthy and happy you got to listen. He said, Jim I've only known you a short time, but he said it's already my honest opinion that for things to change for you, you got to change, that wasn't like the answer I was looking for, that's the answer he gave me and I pass it along to you on this warm summer evening in the united kingdom 2024, for things to change for you, you got to change otherwise it isn't going to change. Before I met Mr self, I used to say I sure hope things will change right, that seems to be my only hope, it isn't going to change, I'm in serious trouble and then I discovered it isn't going to change. So I'm in serious trouble see I can tell you what the twenty first century are going to be like, you have dropped into the right place, I did a seminar one time for Standard Oil executives, and management in Hulu, and we're having a conference Monday, on this big conference table and one of them said to me, Mr on you know, some fairly important people halfway around the world, what do you think these are going to be like.

YOU GOT TO CHANGE FOR CHANGE TO COME PAGE 7.

I said gentlemen I do know, the right people I can tell you, so they all listen very carefully. And I said gentlemen based on my wide experience, I can really honestly say to you in my opinion, in the twenty first century it's going to be about like it's always been, aren't you glad you came that's inside, I don't pass that around just everywhere of course, I said that to make a point, but I also said it because it's accurate, it's going to be about like it's always been to change it comes in and then what it goes out. For 6 1/2 thousand years, that we know our recorded history, and long before that, so it is not going to change, it turns dark 6 1/2 thousand years, see it is not likely to change and we're not to be startled by that. And if the sun goes down then guys what has happened, what has happened it means he hasn't been here long. It always goes down about this time, you got to talk to somebody besides me right. It gets like that it turns dark in rotation, the next season after fall is what winter prey tail how often does winter follow fall every year regularly for the last 6 1/2 thousand. We know see it is not going to change. Now some winters are long, and some are short, and some hard and some are easy. But they always come right after falls, it isn't going to change, sometimes you can figure it out sometimes, there's no way to figure it out sometimes, it goes well sometimes, it gets into not sometimes, it sails along sometimes, it gets in reverse see that's not going to change. The last six thousand years, reads like this, opportunity mixed with difficulty, that's how it reads, it is I'm going to change, coming in says well if it isn't going to change, how will my life ever have changed. Answer when you change and whether I am talking to high school, kids, or business executives my message is always the same, and it goes like this. The only way it gets better for you, is when you get better. Let me give you the four major lessons in life to learn, or majors it's good to study the majors, in our weekend seminar We keep some people don't do well because, they major in minor things you've got to be on the lookout, at the end of every weekend, of every month, you got to check and make sure you're not spending major time, on minor things. We go through that whole series majors, and minors. Now let me give you 2 phrases before we get to the four majors. This will set it up and you will see where I'm going, two key phrases for your notes here's, the first one life and business is like the changing seasons, that's the first phrase life and business is like the changing seasons the best ways to describe life it's like the seasons. Frank Sinatra sings life is like the seasons. Now here is the second race, especially important you cannot change the seasons, but you can change yourself, you can't change the seasons, but you can change yourself.

YOU GOT TO CHANGE FOR CHANGE TO COME PAGE 8.

And see that's how life gets better for you, not by chance, but by change. Now here are the four major lessons in life to learn, here they are #1 learn how to manage the winters math, lesson one they come right after falls, regularity. So long and summer shorten, summer harden summer easy, but they keep coming, you must learn to handle the nights, they come right after days, you must learn to handle difficulty, it comes right after opportunity, you must learn to handle recessions, they always follow progressions for the last 6000 years. See it is not going to change, the lesson you must learn is how to manage it, and there are all kinds of winters. The winter when you cannot figure it out, the winter when it all goes smash, the winter when it turns belly up, the winter when it will not work, when you run out of money and you've got a broken heart, and so those are winter times result. When your heart is smashed in one thousand pieces, typically low your prayers seem to go no higher, than your head it is wintertime. Barbra Streisand sings, be so natural to talk about forever, but used to bees don't count anymore, they just lay on the floor, do we sweep them away, you don't sing me love so then you don't say you need me, and you don't bring me flowers anymore, song of winter let's see the discipline that's come, those are normal that's part of life. But the question is how you manage it, how do you manage the coming winters and the disappointments in the down times. Well, you cannot get rid of January by tearing it off the calendar, but here is what you can do you can get stronger, you can get wiser, and you can get better. The winters will not change, but you can and that's how life changes for you. I thought I understood when it was winter, I used to wish it were summer, I did not understand, but it was hard I used to wish it were easy. I did not know and then

Mr show gave me, a part of his unique philosophy. When he said do not wish it was easier, wish you were better, see that triggered my whole life, change risk for less problems, wish for more skills, don't wish for less challenge, wish for more wisdom, that's the key learn how to handle the winters. Listen to learn how the ticket vantage of the spring, is called opportunity, an spring follows winter what a great place, for if you're going to put it somewhere, that be the place to put it right after winter, and pray tell how often does spring follow winter every year with regularity 6000 years, you can almost count on it see opportunity always comes, days follow nights isn't that so rife. Opportunity follows difficulty, but here's what you must learn to do, underline these two words in that key phrase, take advantage underline those two, must learn to take advantage of the spring, she just because spring rolls around is no sign, you're going to look good come fall, you got to do something with it in fact.

DON'T JUST LET THE SUMMER PAST,

TAKE FULL ADVANTAGE OF IT PAGE 9.

You must get good at one of two things in life, planting in the spring or bacon in the fall, or get somebody to do it for you. See those are about the only alternatives now, here is what else you must do, take advantage of the springs quickly, because there is only a few, just a handful of springs have been handed to each of us. They do not come forever, life is brief so you got to read every book, you can get your firsthand, and what to do with your springs while they are here, and take advantage, they soon run out. The Beatles wrote life is so short, and for John Lennon it was extra short, but life is brief Elton John sings, she lived her life like a candle in the wind. So how are you going to do with your life, you got to get at it, do not just let the springs pass. Here is the third major lesson in life to learn, learn how to protect your crops all summer, you got to take care what you start, sure enough as soon as you planted your garden in the spring. The busy bugs in the noxious weeds are out to take it. The next bit of truth they will take it, unless you prevent it, and that is the third major skill to learn, you have got to learn to prevent the intruder from taking all the good you start, it is one of the challenges. There are two key phrases on the #3, first one all good will be attacked on this planet, not the next one we get to, but on this one all good will be attacked. Every garden will be invaded, not to think so is naïve. And here is the second phrase, all values must be defended, political values, social values, community values, family values, marriage values, friendship values, business values, every garden must be tended all summer. Third major lesson to learn, how to reap in the fall without complaint, turn the reap come harvest time without complaint. Take full responsibility for what happens to you, it is one of the highest forms of human maturity, accepting full responsibility, it is the day you know you passed from childhood to adulthood. The day you accept full responsibility in another note, learn to reap in the fall without apology, without apology if you do well, and without complaint if you do not maturity. I used to have that extensive list of reasons, why I was not doing well explain, otherwise you are going to look bad. I have this funny list called reasons, for not looking good, I used to blame the government, I mean you believe that or not, it was at the top of my list, I had electric second to none.

EVERYTHING CAN HAPPEN PAGE 10.

The government that was on the list is to blame, taxes look what you got left after they take everything, expect you to do well, that was normalised prices that was easy, you walk into the supermarket, with $20 come out with a little half bag. I had that I used to blame the weather, I blame the traffic, I used to blame my car, I blame the manufacturers, I used to blame the company, I blamed company policy, I used to blame the training programme in my negative relatives. They were always putting me down, play my cynical neighbours, they are just selfish, looking out for themselves, will not loan you money, they are only list it is to blame. The economy I blame, the community good list for not doing well, is not it I thought it was good. I will never forget one day, very kindly was also very blunt exception, there is a lot of things out of Mr B, had been blunt. Monday was a curious look on his face, he said Jim just out of curiosity, tell me how come you have not done well up until now. Excellent question I thought well, so I won't look too bad, I'll go through my list, and this list I just gave you, I put that on here and he was very patient with me, go through the whole thing, the government, the weather I went through this whole thing. When I finished, he looked my list over very carefully, he said Mr, one big problem with your list, you made on it, all real when I went to work for him, a few months later, I learned very quickly to tear up my list, reasons for not doing well, and I threw it away and I got me a fresh piece of paper. And I put one word on it, there is a Black heritage spiritual that says, it is not my mother normal father normal brother, Norma's sister. But it is me oh Lord standing in the need of prayer, see I used to blame everything outside, and then let me give you a little philosophy, that helped turn my life around. It is not what happens determines the quality, or the quality of your life, it is not what happens, and the reason is, because what happens, happens to about everybody no different. The sun went down on all of us last night, a common event a happening and I found out that, the same things can happen to two different people, one gets rich in one stay poor, why is that it's because it's not what happens, but rather it's what you do, that changes everything. So that is a key phrase, it's not what happens, it's what you do. What happens is about the same, you might put that in print this here, saying what people do that is what's different, anything can happen. Everything can happen, I have heard all the stories, I've been one of the stories. We could all tell stories all night long, what happenings anything can happen, have you heard of Murphy's laws, anybody heard of Murphy's laws, they must have had look at these logs if anything can go wrong it will these laws, he was not one of the great positive speakers of the day.

WHAT CAN YOU DO IN THE WORLD PAGE 11.

Anything can go wrong, everything can go wrong for sure, I have fallen out of the sky so many times, once to that end of a couple of million devastating took my wallet, survive that one. I was not all that much, but it was all I had, it is much when it is all you have got, if you got 32GO you got one left, you are not looking that bad. But when it all goes has anybody been there, when it all went anybody come on rescue, liars we have all been there. When it all went used to be a long time ago, when you ran out of money, got the zero you were all through it, now you can whistle right on by zero, that is what they will do those are the happenings. Everything can happen anything can happen, but it is not the happenings, it is what you do about it. But you do not understand the disappointments, I have had come on everybody has had their share disappointments, are not extraordinary gifts reserved for the poor. Everybody has the difference is what you do, about it is not the latter, I used to blame the weather, and I discovered it rains on the rich. So, see that will help two men wake up, one morning as a rainstorm on one looks out his window, sees the rainstorm and he say, wow what a storm with weather like this. They cannot expect you to go out and make sales, he stays home same morning. The other guy looks out his window, sees the same storm says wow, what a storm but he said, you know what with weather like this what a wonderful day to Brighton, make sales list everybody will be home, especially the sales. Now your life works out it is not what happens it is what you do. So, here is one of the key questions of the evening, starting tomorrow what you are going to do, that will make a change in your life's. Direction question what you are going to do, starting tomorrow that will be effective, if you do not do something starting tomorrow, that will be effective. Guess what it's going to be the same and see that way you can guess what the next five years are going to be like, look at the last five, the next five are going to be like the last five, or less your major key tomorrow changes it all or change a little or change something or don't change. Its choice time, you can do whatever you want, it is nice to know any day you wish you can change your whole life what can you do start tomorrow will make a difference, question can you do with economic chaos massive disappointment, what can you do with a broken heart, what can you do in the world. Work so if I had a word with you tonight, one-on-one just you and me, I think my personal advice to you would be, this year 2024 reach down inside you, and produce some more of those remarkable human gifts. They are there waiting to be utilised, and then change anything for you, you want to change to do that because you can change, if you don't like how, it is for you change it.

If it does not suit you change it, if it does not, please you change it, if it is not enough change it, and I challenge you to do that, because you can change. See you do not ever have to be the same again, after tonight only by choice, if you do not like your present address change it, you are not a tree personal development, let us get down to the nitty gritty. What does it take to really make the changes starting tomorrow. Philosophical pronouncement I know that it takes more than enthusiasm, that we are hearing a lot about enthusiasm these days. But we are still here on the old cliches, of the right to be enthusiastic, enthusiastic let us see that is not going to help after you have leaked about. There are some things you got to do, or it isn't going to change, all excited about lifting 200 lbs, till you get to the gym, and then you need a new excitement, and the new excitement is called discipline, major step to human progress, discipline if there's one thing to get excited over that's it get excited over your ability, to make yourself do the necessary things. What did you make yourself do starting tomorrow, that would change it all. Now see that is exciting on any given day, you can massively change the direction of your life, murder is a clear example that any one person on any given day can forever alter the course of their life, it just happens to be a negative act. But just as sure as you can commit a negative act you can also commit a positive act, and forever alter your life whenever you wish. Now that is excited whatever that might be, that changes your life. The guy finally takes a shotgun to his car, blows out every window, destroys every tyre, puts 100 rounds in this shabby old thing, and he says, I have driven this embarrassing thing for the last time and not only will I never drive it again, nobody else will never drive it, and let's not shuddering things stand there for a while, as a monument to the day, he said today my life changes. Now who can do that anybody, when can you do it whatever day you pick, the key to discipline starts with the little disciplines, get excited over the little disciplines, and get right on those, because those will lead to the big ones. You cannot manage the big challenges in life, and less you take on the little ones. Make a list of all the things you can do, right on those discipline yourself, for those both for the results and for the muscle and for the practise. So, when life hands you some big challenges, will be ready you will have the muscle, let us see if you do not have the small ones, you can take care of the big ones.

Here is what else it takes for life change, self-motivation key phrase, self-self-motivation, so we call itself motivation, it is really the only thing there is you got to motivate yourself. Because I found out you cannot change people, they can change themselves. But you cannot change him or know some I have tried, let us see it will not work. People must change themselves; I learn some of those lessons early, I build a little sales organisation, way back in those early days, I am 25 and I had some nice people. I said I am going to make these people successful, if it kills, me I almost died, you cannot do that. See I discovered this good people are not trained, their fans you find good people, you do not make him good, you find them good training, really is for the purpose of finding good people, you do not need much instruction for a good person. The two-explaining means, you got the wrong, so you got to find the right people, which is the key to getting a good job. But one of the major things, we learn in management, management lesson 1, don't send your ducks to eagle school', Bause I won't help, I mean I'm telling you won't help no matter how good your skill is, and the legal battle, illegal had until you won't help it, won't help and tell your schools did any good right is when it's over right. But Douglas break first rabbit and makes him a friend you say, no anyway so, it takes self-motivation to really alter your life, and you do not want to give self-motivation away to somebody else and make it somebody else motivating. You the guy says boy, if somebody just come by and turn me on what if they do not show up, see you got to have a better plan for your life OK. Now if you are excited and you're ready, to your life, your personal change, let me give you 3 steps to start life change, which can change your lifestyle. Everything can change, here's the steps #1 find out how things, the first key to doing better, find out to change your library, you need ideas, there isn't anything an idea can't change, and so for me the major problem is lack of an idea, not a problem at first. I did not have any money, I said to Mr sharp, I do not have any money, he said that is not a problem. Now see up until then, I always thought it was, I was confused he said no the problem is lack of an idea, on how to create money and wealth, it is not like a money, it is lack of ideas. So if you get the idea, so you can change anything, now to get ideas you need a constant study ,of finding out, also said when you find out something that works, put the information in your journal, don't use your head for a filing cabinet, put it in your journal. So that you can do the next best thing, repetition go over it and if you repeat it, go but sure enough someday some mysterious day. The idea takes root starts to grow, and shows up in your bank account, and your dress and your personality and your lifestyle.

CURIOSITY PAGE 14.

Capture the ideas in your journal, find out how things work, shocking this word for my life change. He said study great word, if you wish to be successful, study success, if you wish to be happy, study happiness, if you wish to be wealthy, study wealth. Do not leave it to chance, make it a study some people just go through the day with their fingers crossed, see that will do it. You have got to study the things that can change, your economic social spiritual personal life. Now here is a qualifying race and will have several of these qualifying phrases throughout December. You may not be able to do all, you find out I understand that you may not be able to do all, you find out, but you should find out all you can do. See you do not want to wind up at the end of your life and discover that you have lived only 110th of it and the other nine tents, went down the drain not for lack of opportunity for lack of information. So that's number one, find out how things work, now here is the best human virtue, for finding out curiosity make a note of that curiosity, be curious you might add a word to it, that will help childish curiosity. Oh well kids do it they want to know something bad enough, love you that is the phrase they can ask thousand questions, you think they're through they got another thousand, they'll drive you to the brink, it's a virtue when you got to be like a child. Christ the expert teacher said, unless you can become like little children, you might as well forget it, you do not have a prayer excellent advice, you got to be like children. Four ways to be like a child, number one's curiosity, #2 is excitement get excited like a child over your ability to make yourself do anything for change, adults are two sceptical informed distrust just as a child is spiritual, but the rewards are incredible. So be like a child now, if you're curious let me give you three ways to find out how to change anything, any life direction any dimension here's three ways to find out, how to change anything number one is, to read become a good reader, all the successful people I know and work with around the world, they're all good readers. Curiosity drives into read; they got no they just read become a good reader. Now that is my opinion, listen to the other lectures and listen to me, and make up your own mind, do not be a follower, be a student OK. I say really for life change you Gotti read one way to learn is from your own experiences but another way to learn is from other people's, experiences see one book might save you five years, you read it, it is an older book on how to be stronger.

IGNORANCE IS POVERTY PAGE 15.

I see previous speaker, leader have a better effect, on other people develop your personality, did you know those books on that and people do not read them, how would you explain that, and they can read. Did you know that hundreds of successful people, have authored their stories in books, and they wrote down how they did it, and people do not read it. How would you explain that the guys busy, you know you get tide up, the guy says well yes you work where I work, but the time you struggle home it is late. You got diesel by to suffer watch little TV, get to bed you can't sit up half the night reading, reading, and the guys behind on his car payment good worker hard worker sincere, but you got to be better than sincere, and work hard otherwise at the end of your life, you'll wind up cold Stony Brook. You got to be better than a good worker, you got to be a good reader. The entire world is governed by laws, the universe in fact laws, we call it the law of electricity, we call it the law of gravity. There are mathematical laws, there's physical laws, between velocity laws, agricultural laws. There's all kinds of laws, now that we find ourselves on the spinning planet, you just have to learn what I call the setup, learn the setup lies set up, now we didn't set it up, we're here so you got to learn it and we should learn this set up for two basic reasons. Number one to keep from getting hurt. it's one of the major reasons for learning, so you won't get hurt, the economically socially personally you can get hurt, just not knowing entrance is not blessed ignorance is poverty ignorance is tragedy you got know where you're going to get hurt, it's good to know not to walk up A10 Storey window. But that's information, I did not know he walks out Louise dead at the bottom somebody says, well the point I did not know you Gotti know. Well, your goanna gets hurt, you do not have to like the setup, I do not ask him to like how it is, that is not what is important. But it is important to learn how it is OK, so you do not have to like it. But you should learn it that is what I tell the kids right make sure you get the information, what you think about it that is what you are going to do with it that will soon, be up to you. But make sure you get it, see there is nothing worse than being stupid. I mean not having money is bad, but being stupid is idiot, it looks bad is being broken stupid right that's about the end of the world. I mean there isn't anything much worse than that unless you're sick, sick broken stupid I mean that is it right, there's nowhere else to go so make sure you get the information it's key you don't have to like it, but learn it lifts up in the sky hangs there for a little while cuts loose, comes crashing down boom shakes the ground, for five months and then this big monstrous thing, let's back up in the sky pains, or for little while cuts loose again.

VITALITY PAGE 16.

Comes crashing down the ground for five months, it just keeps doing it this big monster slaying, lifting, and then crashing down. Oh, now you might come along one day, and say that has got to be a stupid arrangement, which is OK you are entitled to your opinion. But the first thing you should learn to do is get out from under it that's number one, you might have a great moral argument, you might want to shake your finger at this guy. But do it from over there right, so you do not get smashed it is called your basic smart. So, #1, learn so you will not get hurt whether you like it or not, learn now here is the second reason for learning the set up to benefit, it is called the plus of life and that is what life is right both minus and plus. The minus tragedy heartache misery failure unhappiness, but life is also happiness prosperity good feelings, so here is the key learn to get on the good side, of the way things work, now there is two of the basic laws, and we will take our break these they come from the Bible. Now again I'm an amateur OK, when it comes to the Bible, I'm not a pro, so you'll start to have to take my way of putting it the law of use, the log use and it goes something like this whatever you don't use, you lose, lack of use causes loss on this planet. But on this one if you tyre onto your body leave, it there long enough you will never use it again, it is over for the arm now, may not be over but it is over for the arm. The only way to keep the use of this arm is what if you quit, you lose automatically they do not bring it up for a vote, lose automatically when now you quit the same thing that goes for your arm, goes through your brain mentality. The same thing goes for all the human virtues ambition, unused declines strong feelings, unused diminish it does not grow it diminishes faith unused decreases it is a law vitality, unused diminishes energy unused decreases. Well, I'm gone save up my energy, you can't do that just like trying to save today, put it on the end of the year, so you can't do that they'll come take away, you don't use today what its lost workplaces are tomorrow to make up for it. See that is foolish you could have done that anyway today, unused is lost a talent unused is lost and ability, unused as last. So, here is one of the key expressions of the evening, take a new inventory of yourself, starting tomorrow new project, take a new inventory and make sure that all your talent and ability, and mentality and ingenuity and vitality, and strong feelings courage. Make sure that all you have got being used, otherwise you lose now.

THOSE WHO HAVE MORE, MORE WILL BE REQURIER PAGE 17.

One of the best illustrations of the law of use, is a Bible story called the parable of the talents. The talent story interesting story, if you have not read it in a while, just review it is a delightful story an ancient story. Says there was a master with three servants, he got him together one day and he said to the street, I've got these talents in those ancient days, a talent was a measure of gold, and he said to the three servants, take these talents and see what you can do with them, while I'm gone. He said I am taking a journey I will be gone for a while, when I come back, we will get together go over the book. See how you did, he said here is five of these talents for you, is to open for you and here is one for you. What the master said take those talents, see what you can do with them, when I come back, we will get together we will go over it up this servant said OK master, takes off according to the ancient story. The master comes back from his trip, when he gets back he gets the three servants together and as he said, he would he asks how did it go with those talents, your five what happened, that servant said well, you gave me and I put him to work at first, but he said things finally got rolling and he said I poured it on and he said, my talents grew to 78910 he said I doubled my talents from 5 to 10 books posho, master said one heck of a job. He said I gave you 2 talents what happened, that servant said about the same thing happened to me, I put those two talents to work corded on they grew to three, and then to four he said I doubled my talents from two to four books will show master said well-done. He said I give you one talent what happened that servant said,, well I took the talent you gave me and I carefully wrapped it an I dug a hole and buried it, and he said fortunately nobody got it and he said I knew you were going to be here today. So, I dug it up here it is safely wrapped, I did not lose it according to the ancient story. The expert said take that talent away from him, and give it to the man that is, got now you might say well I don't like that arrangement. The poor guys only got one talent, he's already got 10, they want to be more forever I didn't ask you to like it, but this one I would ask you to learn, because it simply means whatever you do not employ, you forbid it's a loss. So learn well a lot of use now, here's the second one, second law from the Bible, listen we've heard since we were small, I'm sure it's called the love sowing and reaping, in fact we probably heard it so often, we could quote it says whatever you sow, what you salary fairly blunt, hopefully it is clear.

REAP AND SOWING PAGE 18.

Here is my first suggestion on the law of sowing, and reaping, do not try to beat it you might as well try sitting on the sun in the morning, keep it from coming up, you'll have better luck whatever you do. You read now for a fair share of my life, I am a bit Next up on how all this applies, I'm on a lot of things I was Next up on I knew I wasn't reaping too good, that I understood my problem was I was confused about what was causing it. Funny list I thought those are the reasons why it is not working out well, and then Mr self-gave me the clue that helped me figure it all out. He said Mr on I have another answer for you. There is another way to quote this, law little show, you where the problem, is so you can go to work on the right of way, all you need to know is where the problem is, then you go to work on. So, he called me at the law another way, and I found out what the problem was, here is the way you quote the law, whatever you reap is what you sow. Now I knew what my problem was, whatever you read is what you've sown, if you don't like the crop who do you look up, answer whoever planted it And where do you find who planted your crop, answer in the mirror when I finally learned to do come fall was to go to the mirror, that's where you go and necessary you say a few skinny carrots, I got to be unimpressed where were you last spring asleep didn't you read the books, did you break your home. Let me give you 7 key points, to the law sowing and reaping, let's stick right down through the list of seven, and it'll be breakdown seven points to sowing and reaping. Here's part of the philosophy, that really helped me to make some changes in life direction, number one the law sowing and reaping is negative best, number one which simply means if you so bad you reap bad. Now this is kind of third grade, but it does not hurt to go over the basics, if you plant Thistle seed you do not get pumpkins, honest. No, he's looking for pumpkins turn says how come no pumpkins, come on John the laws negative that's outcome. Now here's #2 the last positive quite simply means, if you so good you reap good, you don't get thistles not from pumpkin seeds, well the nature will pull tricks on you, in the corner sneaker pushed Newcastle new plan pumpkin seeds, she won't do that you will get pumpkins from pumpkin seeds, and the reason is because the laws positive. Now here is #3, I got excited when I found out the full dimension of this, see you do not reap what you sow, but rather you always reap much more than what you sow. So, the third keyword is more you don't get back what you put out, you get back much more, and it works all positive and negative, on the negative side it said if you sold to the wind, you reap the whirlwind.

REAP AND SOWING PAGE 19.

So, you got to get ready for that, or you will be naïve, see anybody can whether you will or not see that's the question and here's a good question to ask. We are all buying somebody's plan, the question is who's got you talked into doing what you're doing, who's got you talked into your present plan. Say 10 years from now you will surely arrive, the question is where let's see anybody, if you want to you can go searching for a good plan, picked up and start working it, and sure enough as the time passes as it surely will five years from now .10 years from now then you'll be winding up wearing what you want to wear, driving which you want to drive, living where you want to live, become what you want to become. But now is the time to fix the next 10 years, and who can anybody. Here's number, six the 60 to Sally and reaping, this is levelling with you, now as we promised to do there's one thing better than the truth, and that's the whole truth here is part of the whole truth of love, sowing and reaping. Number six is you could lose, there are times when you just lose no matter what you do, it's that kind of planet you report you. So yes but what does that mean, yes but well the farmer plants his crop industry, takes care of it all summer, loves his family word stand for hours a day 6-7 days a week, is an honourable man confirm he's got a beautiful crop, and he deserves every bit of it. But the day before he sends the crop Bynes, into the field, a hailstorm comes along and beats it all in the ground, which means you lose somebody says well what did he do wrong. Answer nothing it's just that kind of planet, sometimes it's gone hail on your Chrome, an rain on your parade. So you got to get ready for that, or you will be naive that's just part of the life arrangement, and don't press me why I was not. I don't know how it got set up but there's just time sometimes you lose, that's part of life. But now here's #7 70 to Sowing and reaping, and it goes like this it's just another way to quote the same law, and it goes like this yeah. You no so that's just another way to quote the law, if you don't so but you don't read you don't even have a chance. So he looked at your game plan tomorrow, you might come to the quick conclusion, I got to get some stolen going, how true get you some someone going and remember, you've got plenty of time, you've got all the time.

APPRECIEATE THE MOMENT

ALL YOU HAVE IS NOW PAGE 20.

There is some people spend enough TV time to make a fortune, the latest article on television watching in this country, according to the latest article the average television is on in this country, and every household 7 hours a day call the big seven I ask a guy one time what is TV cost he said about $450 I said you forgot to look at the price tag. He said what do you mean, I'm really was a TV watcher, I said that television cost you in my opinion at least $12,000 a year to watch it not to own, its own and it's cheap watching it is what's expensive and I said hey, 12,000 a years too much to pay to watch TV, that's too much pay a little bit not 12,000. And he is the guy that said, I hope ATV never comes OK, Cortana coming off a lot tonight, I realised that, but my time schedule is such that, we just have to sort of give it all to you. Let you sort the rest out, I wish we had plenty of time for questions, and answers in that whole thing. But our time is just limited, we are trying to go through an awful lot, I realise that looks like everybody is getting it, it's about the note taking his crowd, I've seen in a long time incredible anybody have 5 pages, yet anybody fantastic incredible OK. Maybe you heard the story about the preacher down in Texas, southern part of the country, he was an advantage a list back in the horse, and buggy days and he was very good that being evangelist, and a lot of people used to come and hearing preach, and one day he put up his tent in one of these Texas towns, and expected a big crowd as usual, come here increase, and he got there first night in the tent revival, walked in 730 time to start, and to his surprise the tent was empty, he thought well something must be drastically wrong. So, he waited 'til 7:45, nobody showed up, 8:00 zip finally 8:15 one lone cowboy wandered up, on his horse by this horse up outside, came in sat down in the front bench right, waiting for something to happen. The preacher thought well at least, I better go down and talk to the cowboy. So, he walks down talks to the cowboy, and he says cowboy, I'm the preacher, and he said, I don't know what to tell you something's gone wrong he said, this tent was supposed to be full of people, he said I'm embarrassed, he said you're the only one that showed up. He said I really do not know what to do, and the Cowboys said Well, I am not a preacher, so I really cannot tell you what to do. You know he said I am just a cowboy, but he said I know this if I went out to feed my cattle, and only one showed up I had at least feed it.

APPRECIEATE THE MOMENT

ALL YOU HAVE IS NOW PAGE 21.

The preacher thought hey, the cowboy is right, if you have a clever idea to share, you should share it, if there is one or one thousand. So, we got inspired by this conversation, and he jumped up on the platform, started to preach as if that it was full of people, just exploded and he went for an hour and 15 minutes, just kept rolling. Finally, he quit and when he finished, he came down off the platform, talk to the cowboy again says well cowboy what did you think. I am a servant and the cowboy said Well, I am not a preacher so I really cannot tell you know he said. I am just a cowboy, but he said I know this if I were not to feed my cattle, and only one showed up I had feed it. But I would not dump the whole load, on it anyway if it seems like we are dumping the whole load tonight, we are but everybody is doing well, I'm having a good time I REAP AND SOWING PAGE the response here tonight is OK.

The next subject is setting goals, let me show you what turn my life every way, but loose Mr self-dropped this idea on me, changed me completely setting goals. Here is what can easily happen, if you do not set goals, it is easy to let life deteriorate into making a living, instead of designing a life and we all have a choice. Make a living or design a lot it is easy to get trapped, by economic necessity and settle for existence, rather than substance, which is easy. But the best advice I can give you, on how to break out of that trap is to learn how to set goals. Put it to me this way, he said Jim if you had enough reasons, you could do the most incredible things. I never forgot how you put that if you have enough reasons, see reasons will change your whole life Mr Self said to me, said Mr Owen I think you've got plenty of intelligence, you've got plenty of talent, you've got plenty of ability, probably what you lag is plenty of reasons he said. I do not think your current bank balance is a true indication of your level of intelligence, I was happy to hear that he said you are much smarter, than your present bank balance indicates and that is turn out to be true. I was much smarter but of course my first question was well then, why is not it bigger and he said you do not have enough reasons, you have enough intelligence, but not enough reasons. The reasons can change your life, here is what else I found out reasons come first, answers come second, you do not get the answers to do well till you get the reasons. Life as a mysterious way of hanging on all, the answers and only gives them up to the people, which are inspired by reasons. So reasons make the difference in how your life works out, now what are some of the reasons for doing well, let's go through a quick list called reasons for doing well, 1st is personal reasons, some people do well for recognition, some people do well or respect, some people do well for the way it makes them feel, they love the feeling of being a winner, those are good reasons. I have some millionaire friends that keep working 10-12 hours a day, making more millions, and it is not because they need the money, it's because they need the joy and the satisfaction, and the pleasure that comes from being a constant winner. It's not just the money anyway it's the journey, not the money once in a while, somebody says to me boy if I had $1,000,000, I'd never work another day in my life, that's probably why the good Lord sees to it they don't get their million, they've quit OK.

Next is family reasons, some people do extremely well for other people and that's powerful. Human beings can affect each other, sometimes we will do things for somebody else, we will not do for ourselves. We are made that way, I met a man one time who said Mr Alan to do all the things I want to do with my family around the world he said, I got to have at least 1/4 of $1,000,000 a year, my thought incredible could you guys family affecting that much, and the answer is absolutely, how fortunate are the people that find themselves greatly affected by somebody, for personal achievement, and we are affected the writer of a recent song said. if not for you the winter would hold no spring, couldn't hear a Robin saying I just wouldn't have a clue, if not for you so we can be affected, that might be one of the most stimulating reasons to do well, finding somebody when Andrew Carnegie died Lewis little Scotsman, that built the big steel industry. When he died they opened up his desk, and in one of the desk drawers they found a slip of paper on that piece of paper Mr Carnegie had written his goal for his life and he wrote it, when he was in his 20s and on that piece of paper, it said I'm going to spend the first half of my life, accumulating money. I am going to spend the last half of my life giving it all away, want to go he got so inspired by that goal, that the first half of his life. He accumulated $450 million and the last half of his life, he gave it all away good question tonight what has got you turned on, what got you bombed out of sight to get up early and stay up late and hit it all day. Next question what got you turned off when I found the answers to those two questions, my life exploded into change, I finally found out what had me turned off, and I got that cured and then I got me a long enough list of reasons, to turn me on and once the lights went on for me age 25. They have never gone out I pulled out of the sky, a few times but I have never lost that drive to make something unique, out of my life see reasons altered my whole life. Now there is another list of reasons, called nitty gritty, hard little reasons sometimes those little reasons are the most powerful reasons, which can change your life sometimes it does not take much. I now carry several $100 in money clip it's only a few $100, but it was one of those reasons, turn my life around just implying that Mister shelf I heard a knock at the door, I go to the door and there's a little girl standing there, she was tall selling Girl, Scout cookies and she gave me one of the finest sales presentations, I've ever heard special deal several flavours, this whole package is step $2.00 big smile she very politely asked me to buy, and I wanted to big problem I'm broke.

HAVE ENOUGH REASONS PAGE 24.

I don't have two dogs and to this day, I can remember the pain and the embarrassment, I'm a father, I'm a husband, I've been to college, I'm working, I'm 25 I don't have $2.00, and I didn't want to tell her that, for some reason. So, I did what I thought was next best, I lied I said they look I've already bought lots of Girl Scout cookies, I've still got plenty stacked in the house, which was not true, but it seemed to get me off the hook, for the moment she said. Well, gosh that is wonderful thank you very much. And she went away when she left, I closed the door and that was the day I said to myself, I don't want to live like this anymore, I've had with lion and I've had it with being broke, I'm never gone let this happen to me ever again. I promise that day I would work as hard as possible and would always carry plenty it took me a little while, but now I do it, was one of those reasons I carry plenty for two reasons. One is the way it makes me feel, but also in case I bump into another Girl Scout selling cookies right, I am ready I walked out of the Bank of America, one time up in Saratoga CA. Where I used to live 2 girls selling candy right outside the bank, that place goods organisation working for right. I come walking out of the bank this first little girl walks up to me, she said Mr would you like to buy some candy, I said I probably would what kind is it, that's my favourite she said, wonderful I said how much is it, she said it's just two dollars, my thought incredible I said how many boxes of that candy have you got, she said 5 in a little bit candy to. I said how many boxes if you go, she said I have got four. I said that is nine I will take him all reset really. I said yes, it is my favourite. I have some friends I will pass them around. They got so excited promised candy together, I reached in my pocket getting $18.00, when I have the candy and they have the money that first little girl looks up at me, she says Mr you are really something. Can you imagine only spending $18.00 and have somebody look at you in the face and say you are so. Now you know why I carry heavy, I am not gone miss anymore, it was just one of those reasons to change my life, one of my nitty gritty reasons, was budget finance budget finance used to grind my soul way back in those early days. I had fallen for one of those consolidation loans, where you take all your little hard to pay bills put it into one big impossible for baby all right, I would get or five payments behind this one guy used to call me day, and night I don't think they're allowed to do anymore. The run-in charge to ruin my credit balance my family one day, he said we are gone get your card bracketry Linda neighbours, the guy even called me a flake and back in those days, I'm broke I'm pitiful there's nothing I can do about it.

KEEP DREMING PAGE 25.

But I never forgot how the guy treated me, and when I met Mr self, and I got my life started straightened out, and the money started to flow, that was one of my first projects budget finance I poured it on day, and night I finally put all the money together. I owed him, which was considerable, I picked today for the payoff, and when the payoff day came, I put the money in small bills in a big briefcase, and I walked into the budget finance office on Wilshire Blvd in Los Angeles. The guy who harasses me so often his desk was about free bag, I walked out of his desk startling wonder, what I was doing there, it was the first time I'd been there since I bought the money right, without saying a word I opened this briefcase, dump this pile of running all over his desk. I said count it is all there, I will never be back, and I turned around and stormed out. Now that might not be normal, but if you have not tried it you have got to want to turn your life around, all you need is a reason that turns you on one of my dear friends Roberts. If you Bobby used to be a schoolteacher in Lindsay Molly capital, of the world school several years teaching school, one day decided he wanted to get into sales. So, without telling anybody you just up and quit his job, teaching school and jumped into sales, when he did his brother last putting down, said Roberts lost his mind had a good job teaching school, he thinks, he's a St he's gone go down the drain, lose everything just put him down. Something fierce Bobby said the way my brother acted, when I got into sales, he said that made me so mad, I decided to get rich, and my question for you tonight is it possible to get rich, man cars wealth is not a matter of intelligence, it's a matter of inspiration. Today Robert happens to be one of my millionaire friends, bobby's rich Frank Sinatra said one time, the best revenge is massive success, list of reasons for inspiration you might not have all, the answers right away. But you can get the answers, if you can get the reasons now, let me give you a little simple formula for goal setting OK. We take two half hours on the weekend for the whole 10-year plan, we do not have time for that tonight, but let me get you started with a little simple formula. Mr self-gave me, and this will be helpful, first I've divided goals into two parts, 1st is long-range goals that's your dreams, your dreams for the next 3510203040 years. The rest of your life your dreams you have got to keep dreaming. Ronald Reagan president said to the joint session of Congress a few years ago the Republic is a dream and if we do not keep dreaming, we will lose the Republic, your better future is a dream for yourself and for your family. Where do you want to go, what do you want to do, what do you want to be, what do you want to see, you have got the keep dreams.

KEEP DREAMING PAGE 26.

There's a Bible phrase that says without dreams and visions, people perish, you've got to have something to go for, it that inspires the heart and the soul dreams from the children of Sanchez, it says take the crumbs from starving soldiers, they won't die, take the bread from hungry children, they will cry, but without dreams, we all will die. You have got to dream, do not lose your dreams for yourself or your future, for your family, the dreams of love and enterprise and travel, and doing things becoming something unique on your journey. Here do not lose your dreams, do some dreaming that is a long-range goal, you got to have those so that's number one. Here is the second part of goals, short-range, short-range goals that your goals for tomorrow, this week, this month, this year. The immediate future we call these confidence builders, because if you set up something short range, go for it, get it last latch onto it work hard accomplish, it that starts building your strong feelings to go for your dreams.

MAKE A LIST OF ALL YOUR GOAL PAGE 27.

Now I divided goals into three categories, here they are the one is economic that is your goals for money, income business profits production economics, make sure you've got your economics well planned; economics plays a major role in everybody's life. Economics is major which means it ought to be meticulously, well planned for tomorrow, this week this month, this year long range, what if you ask somebody tomorrow, if you could see their meticulously, well planned list of economic goals. Probably say a nut, you must be weird. Hey Cortana, what success is success is doing, what the failures won't do make sure you've got your economics well planned, it'll put you in the top 5% one of the key little subjects, we talk about on the weekend is the 7th fundamentals for wealth and happiness, and that's one of them well planned economics it's a fundamental. If you want to do well join the top 5%, anybody in this room can join the top 5% if you will now here be the second category of goals. Things make a list of the things you want and on my list of things, now I put everything little things as well as major things doesn't matter how small it is, it goes on my list I used to just put major things, cars home I don't do that anymore. I now load my list with everything, and the reason is part of the fun of having a list, is checking it off that is it if you can go, got it. got it, whatever it is right. You get into the habit so load up your list, the things you want now when you check off something major celebrate that is an important point to make, celebrate your achievements, live it up have a party when you reach something, you've worked for a while. See we all grow from 2 experiences, one is called the pain of losing, the other one is called the joy of winning. We both amplifying as much as you can, which also means make losing painful, if you set up something fooled around did not get it put it on yourself on the other side. If you did not get it congratulate yourself, self-congratulations are a sign of maturity seeking congratulations is a sign of immaturity. Hey, winning and losing, so that is what it's all about, that's the name of the game. Now some people lead such mediocre lives, at the end of the day, they do not know whether they're winning or losing, they got no clue, guys just going through the day with this finger crossed, there's a better way OK. Here is the third category of goals, personal development but those goals together crystal development goals, that's your goals to be stronger more decisive via speaker, be a leader what are the language all kinds of skills. The whole weekend seminars designed to improve, all your skills, so that you walk away more and that is what you want, the personal development skills that's what attracts, that's what brings good things to your life.

MAKE A LIST OF ALL YOUR GOAL PAGE 28.

The person you become more now; this is quite a package to work on economics things personal development for tomorrow, this week this month this year long range OK, which will get you started. Now here is the simple formula for setting goals, it goes like this, a on your goals that's step one work on him and I put the word work there deliberately, setting goals is playing hard work. I do not want the kids you haven't come here tonight to kill each other; it's work I know it's work that's why a lot of people just let it slide, it's worth many people work hard on their job, but they don't work hard on their future. They just let that slide and the work involved, is making plans, I know most people do not I understand that, but don't let that be you well yeah. You work where I work for the time you struggle home, it's late you got the device Apple Watch little TV, get to bed you can't set up half the night plan and the guys be good worker hard worker sincere. But you got to be better Benson centre working hard, you got to be better than a good worker, you got to be a good plan, or somebody once wisely said the people who failed to plan, or planning to fail, well said so work on your goals. Here Step 2 write your goals down, that is so important I teach my staff around the world, put your goals in your journal, because one of the major people you want to study is yourself. So, here is the list of goals, I put together 3 weeks ago, here's the list of goals that put together two years ago, here's some of the changes I made rearrange, me of my priorities. I scratch these off I put these on, I have gotten this study your accomplishments, study which your desires have put him on paper. Writing down here is another reason for writing your goals down, it shows you're serious about doing better and to do better you get serious, you don't have to be grim, but you must be serious. Everybody hopes things will get better, everybody hopes call people who want to tell you something, it means the future does not get better by hope, it gets better by planning. I used to have the affliction called passive hope, it is an affliction, it's bad probably even worse than that is happy hope. Now that is bad that's bad guys fifty and he's broke and he still smiling, so get serious about your goals, put him on paper write him down. There are all kinds of his goals, manages their goals business goals, financial goals, financial independence goals, family goals. I mean there is so many things to work on this, but if you don't get busy and work on a shirt up. The time will pass and sure enough five years from now, you will wind up where you don't want to be, wearing what you don't want to wear, driving what you don't want to drive, being what you don't want to be, now is the time to fix it.

ASK FOR WHAT YOU WANT PAGE 29.

Here is the third step to your goals, check the size of your goals, and the kinds of goals, how big they are, what kind they are affects you. Here is one of the important phases of the evening, your goals are affecting you or whatever they are your goals affect your handshake, your goals affect your attitude personality, your goals affect the way you walk, the way you talk, the way you dress. All day long we are being affected by our goals. Now some people have goals, but they have such lousy goal, the effect is bad I ask one time what your goals for this month are, the guy said look if I could just scrape up enough money to pay these lousy bills, which was his goal. I am not saying it isn't a goal, it is a goal but it's such a lousy goal, the effect is bad. You do not go out a bit on Monday morning and say oh boy another chance to grab a script, the money to pay my lousy bills, so you do not do that usually I say oh not another Monday, in some people have given up on life. They have joined the thank God it's Friday, how sad those are the same people when life is over, them will say thank God it's oh let me give you a Bible philosophy that teaches how to get whatever you want. That is the title of the next set of notes, how to get whatever you want from the Bible. Now again I am an amateur when it comes to the Bible, I am not a pro but this I can quote, and I think that will be sufficient how to get whatever you want. Here is what it says, if you are ready, it says ask that is it end of notes, ask if there's one art in life to learn extremely well, that's got to be one of them the art of asking. what does ask me to ask me, what do you want, and the formula staggering is it ask and what a God, to investigate, that he says yes. But you work where I work, but the time you struggle home late you got divide this up and watch little TV, get to bed you can't set up half the night ask, I ask and the guys lean. So, you got to be better than a good worker, you have got to be a good asker. Now let me give you 3 key points on asking and receiving this can do it number one asking is the beginning of receiving asking starts, a unique process mental and emotional, I don't even know how it works. All I know is it works, it's like pushing a button and all this machinery starts working I do not know how it just works there's a lot of things you don't need to know, how just welcome some people always studying the roots others are picking the fruit. I mean it depends on what end of it you want in on asking is the beginning of receiving. So, start the process here's #2 receiving is not the problem, receiving is automatic that's true receiving is not the problem, what's the problem failure to ask might be one of your major problems. I don't know check it out the guys oh now I see it, I got up last year and hit it every day, but there's not a scrap of paper with my goals decent work core aspect, so you change that.

YOUR EMOTION PAGE 30.

Here is #3 receiving is like the ocean, there is especially in California it's like an ocean, here success is not in short supply, it isn't rationed, and you stepped up to the window, and it was all gone no it's like an ocean. Here now that's true what's the problem, well some people go to the ocean where the teaspoon, have you got the picture, see what you want to do in view of the size of the ocean, is trade your TSP for at least a bump, and you look better down at the old kids won't make fun of you OK. Now there is two ways to ask it will wrap up goal setting, two ways here's number one, ask with intelligence it did not say ask intelligently, but I am sure it meant that don't mumble, you don't get anything by mumbling. Be clear be specific intelligent asking means how wide, how high how soon when what size what colour how much define what you want and describe what you want that is powerful. And the weekend seminar we instruct girls become like amendment they pull you that direction, and the better you describe them the more they follow. So, ask intelligently, here is #2 ask with faith that is the childish part of the equation, believe you can get what you want like a child not an adult, adults are two sceptical. So, the formula really reads make plans like an adult, and believe in him like a child, and the most incredible things will happen. Try it for 90 days, just try it you can always go back to the old ways, just try it, just 90 days, 90 days. Now here is the last qualifying phrase on goal setting, as we promised to qualify everything and it simply goes like this, remember you will not get everything you want, and we have already studied. The reason for that simply sometimes, it hails on your crop and rains on your parade, it is that kind of planet. So, you will not get everything you want, but if you will work this goal setting formula, you can get plenty for wealth and happiness OK, that's goal setting we use it around the world. We recommend it now maybe it will not work as well for you, as it has for me, I do not know but what if it did, you got to try OK. Here is the last subject today, that turns your life around, let me just quickly give you a list of four emotions, which can change your life, in one day emotions are powerful sometimes it does not take much, to alter your whole life direction OK. Here they are #1 discussed powerful emotion, discussed says I had edit, see that could be the day, the day you can say I have had it, and what do you have it with something small, or something major. The day you can say I've had it, may not be the day it ends, but the day it begins that's what I said when that little girl's got left my door, when I'm 25 I give it a big lie, she leaves I say I don't want to live like this anymore, I've had it with lion and being broke powerful day.

MAKE A DECISION TO CHANGE YOUR LIFE PAGE 31.

finally had it with mediocrity is headed with being a loser, he's finally had it with those awful sick feelings inside, knowing his wife aseptic grocery store looking two cans of beans, one mark 37 cents, one mark $0.39, and the guy sick inside knows his gone buy the 37 cent can, and she doesn't even like the brand. Cortana why she is bought the 37th can, the same terms said the guys stick inside finally says, I've had it being on my knees in the dust looking for pennies, we're not living like this anymore, be the day to turn your life around. But they you can say I've had it; he walks into his closet and rips everything in it to shreds, and says I've worn this embarrassing stuff for the last YEAR, and not only will I never wear it again, but no one also else nowhere commit an act that says I add it. Here's the next one decision and decision making is powerful, and its emotional vessels knots in the pettier stomach right. Waking up in the middle of the night in a cold sweat trying to decide, we sometimes call it inner civil war, what shall I do well for progress, you must decide the best advice I can give you, came from a wealthy friend of mine. Who said if it's easy do it easy, if it's hard do it hard, just get it done, if you went home tonight and in the next few days, cleaned up a whole list of decisions that might produce enough inspiration for the next 10 years. I found this out many times after you've decided getting on with it, is easier than deciding sometimes, decision is the toughest part. Here's the next emotion desire wanting to bad enough, and I don't know how to tell you to want to that's something, you've got to come up with there's two things I know about desire #1 it comes from inside, not outside, you don't send off for it, #2 I know desire can be triggered by something who knows what it might be. Sometimes desire waits and sleeps for something to happen, maybe it's a book, maybe it's a song, maybe it's a sermon, maybe it's a lecture A colon are maybe it's the conversation of a friend happening, an event who knows the best, I can advise I can give you is what I give my staff. It goes like this; welcome every human experience you never know which one is going to turn it all on. The bad experience sometimes from the business experience, comes the greatest awakening. So let down the barriers, take down the walls the same wall that keeps out disappointment, keeps out happiness, let touch you don't let it kill you, but let it touch.

Here's the last one, this was powerful resolve says, I will two of the most powerful words in the language, I will Benjamin Disraeli once said nothing can resist a human real that will stake, even its existence on the extent of his purpose, certainly put I'll do it or die. See that is powerful that could be the day to turn your life around, the world has a strange way of stepping aside, when somebody says I will do it or die. The man says I will climb the mountain, they told me it is too high, it is too far it is too rocky it's too difficult, it's never been done before. But it is mine mountain I will claim it soon, you will see me waving from the top, or dead on the side causse I are not coming back. The best definition I ever got from the word resolve, came from a little junior high girl in foster city CA up north, I'm talking to the junior high kids one day, I looked at kids definitions they come up with beauties I got the word resolved, and I asked who can tell me what resolve means, and I got several hands and they were all pretty good. But the last one was the best little girl, Mr bone I think I know what resolve me, I said darling what do you think it means, she said I think it means promising yourself you will never give up, I said that's it Webster stand aside that is the definition promise yourself you will never give up. I asked the kids how long a baby should try to learn how to walk, how long would you give your average maybe 47 months, how long see anywhere in the world would say you're crazy, my baby is going to keep trying until it learns how to walk, what a man. Now let me show you what triggers all emotions into activity that brings results, and results is the name of the game. Here it is action finally you must do something about how you feel. Christ the expert teacher said, don't just be listeners, be doers the world admires the doers, whatever it takes to get you to try harder read more set your goals and go for it. Here is the next attitude disease over caution. Some people never will have much, they are two cautious. Now you can also be too reckless, but you can also be too cautious, this is called the timid approach to life and my question was always the risk used to drive me right up the world. I used to say what if this happens, it's called the language of the poor lot of this happens, and on top of that if this was to happen, look at the fix I'd be, and I better not try I could always ask myself out then I'll tell you what changed my whole life. When I finally discovered it is all risky, the minute you were born it got risky, if you think flying is risky, wait till they hand you the bill for not trying.

THINK POSSITIVE PAGE 33.

Did you think investing is risky, wait till you get the tab, or not investing. See it is all risky getting married, is risky having children, is risky going into business, is risky investing your money, is risky it is all risky I will tell you how risky life is, you're not going to get out alive frisky. It's gone workout, let's give it a go right that's what it's for give it a go, somebody says yeah, but I'm looking for safety insecurity find that little corner will cover you, with the seat bringing 3 meals a day, will protect you, feed you look after you care for you, we won't let anything happen to you, and you'll probably live to be 100 I'd love to be 100. but what a way to live right, quite a way to live safe and secure don't ask for security ask for adventure, better to live 30 years full of adventure than 100 years safe in the gardener and see it's not important how long you live, what's important is how you live. Here is the next attitude disease we are through this monthly list, in fact we are almost through hang on the next one is pessimism, the deadly disease of always looking on the bad side, the problem side the difficult side checking all the reasons why it can't be done. The poor pessimist leads an ugly life, he doesn't try to figure out what's right, he tries to figure out what's wrong, he doesn't look for virtue, he looks for faults and when he finds him, he's delighted how this is the poor guy looks through the window, doesn't see the sunset. He sees the specs on the wind, and this is the poor guy writing rushes uptake such leaving his senses, this guy rushes up and he says I've got five good reasons why won't work. He is so dumbed he doesn't know all he needs one he's got 5 celesta glasses, always have T to the optimist. The glass is half full quite with the same measure, affect people two diverse ways answer it all depends on how you look at it our lives, are mostly affected by the way we think. Things are not the way they are ,the way we think they are a sexist most there's a subject, we don't have time to get into tonight called better thinking habits, one of the major things MR self-taught me, when I met him he said poor thinking habits, keeps most people poor not poor working habits, most people work hard but they don't think hard. Mr self-self-taught me, that the mind is like a factory mental factory and whatever you think about all day long, pours ingredients into this mental factory, and that is what bills the economic social, financial fabric of your life. He quoted me a Bible phrase that says, as you think so you become, awesome when you talk about poor thinking habits, he had me I used to start the day reading the morning newspaper, I mean you can believe that or not I get a cup of coffee read the paper, I'd load up on wars and riots and murders and stabbings, and killings, and bank robberies, and muggings and car wrecks, and tragedies, I'd even read the back pages.

I like that stuff for some weird reason, I load up on all that when I start the day. You can imagine the kind of days, I used to have you walk around on your financial knees, they call you economic anyway the guy says, I be a great leader wonderful. The first thing we do is following to his house, when we get there, we walk in and check his library. #1 somebody says well why check his library, the reason is because what a man reads pores massive ingredients into his mental factory, and the fabric of his life is built from those ingredients. You would not believe what some people have got in their house to read, you would not believe what are the best up words. I know for a lot of it is clash, can you imagine dumping a bill of rubbish into this mental factory. Every day and coming out with a rich dynamic positive life, it can be done. You might as well try making a cake with cement, the kids back in Denbury Connecticut high school, they are asking me questions when they are talking to the kids, got good questions, these days said to me. Mr on how you build the good life, so you must be wise and careful, what you think about because that starts everything you got. Be wise and careful, I asked the kids what would happen if somebody dropped sugar in my coffee, they said will you be OK, I said what if somebody drops strychnine in my coffee, they said will you be good, I said correct lesson one life is both sugar and strychnine. You Gotti be careful, I said one of my worst enemy drops in the sugar, I said one of my best friends in my accident drops in district 9. They said Well you would be dead I said correct lesson 2, watch your curl, you got be careful. See it does not matter, who hands you the serious stuff it does not matter, where you get the serious stuff, it'll still do its damage on your bank account. Wherever you get it Mr self gave me one of the greatest phrases, when I first met him, when he said gym everyday stand guard at the door of your market, how important stand guard at the door of your mind, and you decide what goes into your mental factory. Do not let anybody just dump anything they want to, in your mental factory because you have got to live with the results OK.

MAKE SURE YOU'R WINNING PAGE 35.

Here is the last disease and we are through with this list in fact, we are through hang on the last subject is very brief. The last disease but this one is deadly engaged in this one indulge in it even slightly, and you might as well forget the future, because it is going to forget you complaining crying griping a Bible word called murmuring. See that'll ace your future spend 5 minutes complaining, and you have wasted 5 and you may have begun, what's known as economic cancer of the bone, surely, they will soon haul you off and or financial desert, and there let you choke on the dust of your own regret. I hope I said that well, so you will not forget it is a deadly disease if you do not think it is bad, ask the children of Israel of Old Testament fame typical of us all. Their story just happened to get in the book, story says children of Israel were slaves, God performed a series of dazzling miracles and got him out, and now they are heading for the promised land. The story heading for the promised land tragedy of the story, they never got there, reason day one they started to complain, they griped about the water they griped about the web. They whined and cried and griped, the food they griped about the leadership they whined and cried, because it was too far, too cold, too hot, too difficult, too miserable, I mean they widen coins and cried for it is finally God, said I bought it cancelled or something like that. The story says they died, in the desert never got the promise land, left which I think means two things, indulge in this long enough you get your future cancelled, and it also means even, God himself can only take so much. Just be on the lookout of the things, which can destroy all the good you start, the war is on, and this evening tomorrow mentally personally socially, economically you got to make sure, you are winning the war,

WHAT IF I'M WRONG

TABLE OF CONTENT

TABLE OF CONTENT

INTERDUCTION

Life is a journey filled with difficulties challenges, and triumphs, it is a constant battle between our inner strength, and weaknesses. While we all aspire to live a life of purpose and resilience. There are habits that often hold us back from reaching our full potential, in this transformative journey we will explore nine habits that make you weak and learn how to overcome them. Using the principles of stoicism and ancient Greek philosophy, founded by Zeno of Citium, in the early third century BC, offers timeless wisdom that can help us, navigate the complexities of modern life stoicism. Teaches us to focus on what we can control, to cultivate virtue like wisdom, courage, self-discipline, and to accept the inevitable challenges of life with grace and resilience. As we delve into these eight habits, remember that self-awareness is the first step towards transformation, by recognising and acknowledging these habits, within ourselves. We can begin the journey of replacing them with stoic principles, which will empower us to lead a life of strength, purpose, and inner peace. Habit #1 procrastination of time epictetus said, the key is to keep Company only with people who uplift you, whose presence calls forth your best procrastination. The act of postponing tasks and responsibilities is a habit that plagues many of us, it weakens our resolve, hinders our progress, and robs us of precious time, which could be invested in personal growth, and meaningful endeavours. The historic remedy for procrastination lies in the concept of carpe diem or seizing the day in stoicism. The focus is on the present moment and making the most of its procrastination, on the other hand is rooted in anxiety, about the future, or the discomfort of the task at hand, to overcome this habit, we must adopt A stoic mindset.

SELF DISCIPLINE PAGE 12.

MANIFEST YOUR IDEA PAGE 13.

www.ingramcontent.com/pod-product-compliance
Lightning Source LLC
Chambersburg PA
CBHW071103290526
45795CB00004B/1631